Asylum

A play

Alec Baron

Samuel French – London
New York – Sydney – Toronto – Hollywood

Copyright © 1990 by Alec Baron
All Rights Reserved

ASYLUM is fully protected under the copyright laws of the British Commonwealth, including Canada, the United States of America, and all other countries of the Copyright Union. All rights, including professional and amateur stage productions, recitation, lecturing, public reading, motion picture, radio broadcasting, television and the rights of translation into foreign languages are strictly reserved.

ISBN 978-0-573-12010-7
www.samuelfrench.co.uk
www.samuelfrench.com

FOR AMATEUR PRODUCTION ENQUIRIES

UNITED KINGDOM AND WORLD EXCLUDING NORTH AMERICA

plays@samuelfrench.co.uk
020 7255 4302/01

Each title is subject to availability from Samuel French, depending upon country of performance.

CAUTION: Professional and amateur producers are hereby warned that *ASYLUM* is subject to a licensing fee. Publication of this play does not imply availability for performance. Both amateurs and professionals considering a production are strongly advised to apply to the appropriate agent before starting rehearsals, advertising, or booking a theatre. A licensing fee must be paid whether the title is presented for charity or gain and whether or not admission is charged.

No one shall make any changes in this title for the purpose of production. No part of this book may be reproduced, stored in a retrieval system, or transmitted in any form, by any means, now known or yet to be invented, including mechanical, electronic, photocopying, recording, videotaping, or otherwise, without the prior written permission of the publisher. No one shall upload this title, or part of this title, to any social media websites.

The right of Alec Baron to be identified as author of this work has been asserted in accordance with Section 77 of the Copyright, Designs and Patents Act 1988.

Other plays by Alec Baron published by Samuel French Ltd
Big Cats
Chimera
Company Come
Dress Rehearsal

A licence issued by Samuel French Ltd to perform this play does NOT include permission to use any copyright music in the performance. The notice printed below on behalf of the Performing Right Society should be carefully read.

The following statement concerning the use of music is printed here on behalf of the Performing Right Society Ltd, by whom it was supplied

The permission of the owner of the performing right in copyright music must be obtained before any public performance may be given, whether in conjunction with a play or sketch or otherwise, and this permission is just as necessary for amateur performances as for professional. The majority of copyright musical works (other than oratorios, musical plays and similar dramatico-musical works) are controlled in the British Commonwealth by the PERFORMING RIGHT SOCIETY LTD, 29–33 BERNERS STREET, LONDON W1P 4AA.

The Society's practice is to issue licences authorizing the use of its repertoire to the proprietors of premises at which music is publicly performed, or, alternatively, to the organizers of musical entertainments, but the Society does not require payment of fees by performers as such. Producers or promoters of plays, sketches, etc., at which music is to be performed, during or after the play or sketch, should ascertain whether the premises at which their performances are to be given are covered by a licence issued by the Society, and if they are not, should make application to the Society for particulars as to the fee payable.

CHARACTERS

Dr Hilde Kirshner, head of the Sanatorium
Secretary
Probation Officer
Metz, a male nurse
Bauermann, a patient
Dr Lisa Morgan, Bauermann's daughter

The action takes place in the Hohlehof Mental Health Sanatorium in West Germany, 1970

ASYLUM

Scene 1

The office of Dr Hilde Kirshner. Germany, 1970

There are notices on the wall in German, and a large calendar from a German pharmaceutical firm with the year 1970 clearly visible. Dr Kirshner, head of the Hohlehof Mental Health Sanatorium in West Germany, is a woman in her fifties, with German thoroughness and efficiency yet with a pronounced sympathetic quality. She is sitting at her desk, wearing a white coat, reading a case history

The secretary enters, a young woman, carrying some files

Secretary (*reluctant to interrupt her*) Frau Doctor . . .
Dr Kirshner (*without looking up*) Yes?
Secretary The Probation Officer from Munich is here.
Dr Kirshner Here? What about?
Secretary About Herr Bauermann.
Dr Kirshner Why? What's Bauermann done?
Secretary Nothing. His year is up next week.
Dr Kirshner Next week? It can't be!
Secretary I've brought his file. (*She opens it and reads*) "Your report should reach the Court no later than October twenty-third, nineteen seventy."
Dr Kirshner That was last week! Why didn't you tell me?
Secretary I . . . overlooked it.
Dr Kirshner (*furious, taking the file*) Ask him to come in.
Secretary Who? Herr Bauermann?
Dr Kirshner No, you dummy! The probation officer!
Secretary It's a woman. I've never seen her before.
Dr Kirshner A woman? Very well.

The Secretary exits

Dr Kirshner examines the file

After a moment, the Secretary shows in the Probation Officer, a rather masculine lady. She is carrying some notes

Probation Officer Doctor Kirshner . . .
Dr Kirshner Please sit down.
Probation Officer (*sitting*) Thank you. About Herr Bauermann. The Court is in session tomorrow and your report will be required. It seems we have mislaid it.
Dr Kirshner I have not yet submitted my report.
Probation Officer It was due a week ago.
Dr Kirshner I have not yet come to a decision. Herr Bauermann has proved to be a very difficult patient.
Probation Officer Difficult? I would have thought you'd be used to that in a place like this.
Dr Kirshner We are. By difficult, I don't mean that he has given us any trouble. Quite the contrary. In fact I've wondered once or twice what he was doing here.
Probation Officer Then what's the problem?
Dr Kirshner The sessions I've had with him have proved most unsatisfactory. I've never managed to get much more than a yes or no out of him and if I ask him anything at all relative to his case he doesn't reply at all.
Probation Officer I thought you people had drugs which, shall we say, encouraged people to talk.
Dr Kirshner I am most reluctant to employ those methods here. I don't believe in them.
Probation Officer Dr Kirshner, may I remind you that this man was sent here by the Court for one year so that you could decide whether it would be safe to return him to normal society. The Court awaits your decision.
Dr Kirshner I have not yet arrived at a decision. I can make no recommendation either way.
Probation Officer Frau Doctor, according to my information here, Bauermann has been convicted three times of vicious and motiveless attacks on people. Surely the man must be of unsound mind.
Dr Kirshner You've never met Bauermann, have you?
Probation Officer No.
Dr Kirshner Yet you've already come to a conclusion.
Probation Officer But the man attacked a subordinate with an axe

handle, a foreman in the factory where he was working! The foreman knew of no reason why he should have been attacked, they hardly knew each other. Surely ——
Dr Kirshner (*interrupting*) I read the transcript of the trial. I am quite familiar with what he did. What interested me was that he refused to say anything either to his solicitor or in Court.
Probation Officer He went to prison nevertheless!
Dr Kirshner Didn't seem to help him, did it?
Probation Officer Some time later he attacked a schoolteacher in the street. They didn't know each other at all! The man is obviously prone to sudden brainstorms of some kind.
Dr Kirshner And he went back to prison again!
Probation Officer (*referring to her notes*) Yes, and attacked a prison warder.

Dr Kirshner shakes her head, as if not understanding why he did this

Bit him. Viciously.
Dr Kirshner Prison doesn't seem to be the right treatment for Herr Bauermann, does it?
Probation Officer (*getting heated*) Frau Doctor, prisons are equipped to punish these villains, not to treat them!
Dr Kirshner Yes I know, and you seem to have punished this "villain" three times.
Probation Officer Rightly or wrongly the Court sent Bauermann to you. I am not responsible for the Court's rulings, nor do I always agree with them. I am merely required to carry them out. I have come for your decision. Is it safe to set Bauermann free, or does he stay here for the rest of his life?
Dr Kirshner (*standing*) The Court allowed me a year in which to decide.
Probation Officer The year is nearly up!
Dr Kirshner There is still one week.
Probation Officer With respect, Frau Doctor, we need to know now. There are procedures . . .
Dr Kirshner Your procedures will await my decision. Please convey that message, will you. Good-afternoon.

Reluctantly, the Probation Officer leaves, annoyed at being dismissed so abruptly

Dr Kirshner sits down, looks at Bauermann's file again, then presses a button on her desk

The Secretary enters

Dr Kirshner Would you ask Metz to come and see me.
Secretary Yes, Frau Doctor. (*She turns to go, then stops*) You upset that Probation Officer, didn't you? She was furious!
Dr Kirshner The Courts can't expect me to take their failures off their hands, even though their prisons are full. I won't do it! Not without a struggle. Now, if you'll get Metz for me.
Secretary Yes, Frau Doctor.

The Secretary exits

Dr Kirshner dials a number

Dr Kirshner (*on the phone*) Ah Helga—I'll be a little later than I said tonight. Please tell Herr Kirshner to eat without me. I'll be home as soon as I can.

She puts the phone down

Metz, a male nurse, enters. He is a large, powerful man

Metz You wanted to see me, Frau Doctor?
Dr Kirshner Yes. Sit down, Metz. (*He sits*) It's about Bauermann. How has he been behaving?
Metz No trouble at all. Not a bit like the others. Very quiet man.
Dr Kirshner Depressed?
Metz (*uncertain*) Mmmm... less than most.
Dr Kirshner Does he appear to be—rational?
Metz Oh, he's rational all right, but I've no doubt he could have another attack at any time.
Dr Kirshner You've no doubt? Why have you no doubt?
Metz Well, he wouldn't be here in the first place unless... I mean I don't know much about Bauermann but they don't put people in places like this without their being dangerous, do they?
Dr Kirshner Has he talked to you?
Metz What about?
Dr Kirshner Oh, generally. Do you find him... easy to talk to?
Metz I don't get all that near to him if I can help it.
Dr Kirshner (*displeased*) Indeed!

Asylum

Metz I mean — I don't turn my back on him, not after what *he's* done! He keeps to himself — reads.
Dr Kirshner Reads?
Metz He asks for a book now and again, borrows my newspaper when I've done with it, you know.
Dr Kirshner I have to come to a decision about him. I've no wish to put a man away, probably for life, if there's the slightest hope that ... on the other hand I have to consider the danger to the public.
Metz Of course.
Dr Kirshner (*deliberating for a while*) Would you bring him in, Metz. If I tell him of the decision I have to take, frankly, and the prospects, it might persuade him to open up a little.
Metz Yes, Frau Doctor.

Metz exits

Dr Kirshner continues looking at the papers. She then closes the file, sighs and taps on the desk with a ruler, in thought, with her back to the door

> *There is a knock on the door and Metz comes in with Bauermann. He is a white-haired man in his sixties; wiry. His face is thin and lined, but with a gentleness about him and an occasional look on his face as if he was pleading for help*

Metz Herr Bauermann, Frau Doctor.
Dr Kirshner Thank you, Metz. Would you leave us.

Metz looks at her doubtfully and doesn't move

> Thank you, Metz.

Metz leaves

> Sit down, Herr Bauermann.

Bauermann sits

> (*After a pause, smiling*) How are you feeling?

Bauermann (*shrugging*) Thank you.
Dr Kirshner (*walking to the front of the desk and resting on it*) Herr Bauermann, your case is about to come up for review. It falls to me to decide whether it would be safe to let you go free. (*Pause*) Do I have to tell you what the alternative might be?

Bauermann does not reply

Do you want to spend the rest of your life here?

She waits for a reply, looking for a sign of emotion in his face, but there is none. She goes behind her desk and sits

Herr Bauermann, I would like to help you. That is what I am here for, believe me. I am not a gaoler. But I cannot help you if you will not co-operate with me.

There is a long pause. She looks at him closely

Bauermann What do you want me to do?
Dr Kirshner I simply want you to talk to me.
Bauermann About what?
Dr Kirshner About yourself.
Bauermann Not why!
Dr Kirshner What do you mean, "not why"?
Bauermann Everybody asks me why. I don't know why.
Dr Kirshner There is very little in your papers about your family. No-one has been to visit you. Have you any family?
Bauermann Nobody.
Dr Kirshner Parents?
Bauermann They died a long time ago.
Dr Kirshner What did your father do?
Bauermann (*impatiently*) How does it help?
Dr Kirshner What?
Bauermann So you know what my father did! How does it help? What's it got to do with me?
Dr Kirshner How old were you when you married?
Bauermann Does it matter?
Dr Kirshner It says here your wife is dead.
Bauermann And my son.
Dr Kirshner Yes, it says that too. What was your son called?
Bauermann (*quietly*) Eckhart.
Dr Kirshner Eckhart?
Bauermann Yes.
Dr Kirshner Where did it happen?
Bauermann In Munich. We lived in Munich then.
Dr Kirshner When?
Bauermann During the war.

Dr Kirshner (*looking at his papers*) An air-raid, wasn't it?
Bauermann You know. Why are you asking?

Dr Kirshner closes the file. There is nothing more there

Dr Kirshner How old was your son?
Bauermann In nineteen forty-four?
Dr Kirshner When it happened.
Bauermann He was ... five. (*He smiles*) A bonny, loving child.
Dr Kirshner Where were you, when it happened.
Bauermann I worked.
Dr Kirshner Where?
Bauermann (*impatiently*) What does it matter? I worked.
Dr Kirshner What did you do?
Bauermann Germany was at war!
Dr Kirshner Were you a soldier?
Bauermann I'm an engineer! I made armaments, what else? Armaments are more valuable than soldiers.
Dr Kirshner I noticed you've had several different appointments since the end of the war—Hamburg, Aachen, Coblenz ...
Bauermann I ... didn't like Munich any more. I moved away.
Dr Kirshner Herr Bauermann, did you never think of marrying again?
Bauermann No.
Dr Kirshner Why not?
Bauermann Please! No whys! No why nots!
Dr Kirshner This schoolteacher you attacked—it says in your papers that you didn't even know him.

Bauermann does not reply

He was just walking along the street with a class of children. Can you think of any reason for attacking him? (*She waits*)

Bauermann sits looking straight ahead, without reaction

Before you did it, were you feeling all right? Did you have any pain? Can you remember? (*Pause*) Were you feeling depressed? Lonely? Badly done to? (*Pause*) Herr Bauermann, people don't suddenly attack total strangers for no reason at all. Try to recall—did you have a headache?

He does not answer

She moves across the room

Herr Bauermann, I have to come to a decision about you. If you refuse to co-operate ...
Bauermann I am not sure that ... I want to leave this place.
Dr Kirshner I see. You feel that you might be tempted to ... to attack someone again?

Bauermann does not reply

I have to protect society you know.
Bauermann Protect society? From me? (*He smiles*) No, I wasn't thinking of that. I was thinking that perhaps your asylum could protect me from society.
Dr Kirshner (*deciding on a different approach*) Was your marriage a happy one, Herr Bauermann?

His face softens

Have you got a picture of your wife?

He doesn't react

A photograph ... of your wife.
Bauermann (*far away*) Eh? Oh! Yes, I have a photo.
Dr Kirshner Would you mind if I saw it?

He produces a shabby wallet and takes out a worn picture. Dr Kirshner looks at it and smiles

What a happy picture! The two of you, with the baby. Is this Eckhart?
Bauermann Eh? Er, no. Wait, let me see.

She shows him the photograph

Yes, Eckhart, Eckhart.
Dr Kirshner (*returning the picture*) It must have been a terrible blow.

He shrugs

But thousands of people lost their families, their homes, in almost every city in Germany. They don't all go attacking strangers, Herr Bauermann.
Bauermann Have you finished with me?

Asylum

Dr Kirshner Herr Bauermann, you must help me to help you.
Bauermann I would like to go back to my room.
Dr Kirshner (*ignoring him*) Tell me, where were you born?
Bauermann What *difference* ...
Dr Kirshner Munich? Was it Munich?
Bauermann (*after a moment; forbearing*) Munich, Munich.
Dr Kirshner Did you have brothers or sisters?

Bauermann does not answer

Herr Bauermann, *please* co-operate with me.
Bauermann A sister. I had a sister. What's that got to do ...
Dr Kirshner (*persistent*) Where is she?
Bauermann Dead.
Dr Kirshner I'm sorry. Did you get on well with your father?

He looks at her as if she was crazy, then sighs as if to say what a waste of time

Bauermann Of course.
Dr Kirshner And your mother?
Bauermann Sure. Sure.
Dr Kirshner How old were you when you first had a sexual relationship?
Bauermann If you don't mind, Doctor, I'd like to go back to my room. (*To himself*) When did I first have a sexual relationship!! (*To Dr Kirshner*) Do you know how old I am?
Dr Kirshner Herr Bauermann, there are many things which might not seem important to you but might have some significance to a trained practitioner. If I am to help you I should be obliged if you would just answer my questions, as truthfully as you are able. Now. Can you remember your first sexual encounter?
Bauermann (*standing up*) May I go back now?

She looks at him for a long time as he stands, patiently. She goes back to her desk and presses the button

Metz enters

Dr Kirshner Take him away!

Music, quietly

Metz takes Bauermann's arm and they leave

Dr Kirshner sits down and makes a gesture of extreme frustration. The Lights fade as the music swells

SCENE 2

Dr Kirshner is working at her desk. The music fades

The Secretary enters

Secretary Dr Morgan is here.
Dr Kirshner Good.

Dr Lisa Morgan, a smartly dressed woman in her late thirties, is shown in. She is very English in her manner and appearance and a rather pompous person

The Secretary exits

Dr Morgan Dr Kirshner?
Dr Kirshner (*standing up*) Yes.
Dr Morgan Lisa Morgan. How do you do.

They shake hands

Dr Kirshner I see you haven't forgotten the German language.
Dr Morgan One never forgets one's mother tongue.
Dr Kirshner Won't you sit down, Dr Morgan.
Dr Morgan Thank you.

They sit

Dr Kirshner It's extremely good of you to come so promptly.
Dr Morgan I flew over immediately, of course. Are you sure this man *is* my father?
Dr Kirshner I believe so.
Dr Morgan Did he tell you about me?
Dr Kirshner No he didn't.
Dr Morgan Then how on earth did you locate me? I lost contact with him thirty years ago. He just seemed to have disappeared. My letters were returned, marked "not known". We assumed he had died.
Dr Kirshner Did you have a brother?

Asylum

Dr Morgan Yes, I did.
Dr Kirshner What was his name?
Dr Morgan Eckhart.
Dr Kirshner To be truthful, he didn't tell me he had a daughter, only a son. He showed me a photograph of his wife and child. When I asked him whether the child was Eckhart he said it wasn't. Then he quickly changed his mind and said it was. I just thought that there might possibly be another child.
Dr Morgan But how did you find me?
Dr Kirshner Your father took the photograph from a wallet. Later I thought I'd like another look. He always slept with the wallet under his pillow but he'd had a sleeping pill so there was no difficulty. There was very little in the wallet—it had been carefully examined before of course—a small round locket, a wedding ring, two or three photographs of your mother. One of the photographs was of your mother with another woman and on the back of it I could just make out the name Morgan Cant and a number. I guessed it might be a telephone number. We tried to trace this Mr Cant without success, then I had the wild notion that Cant might stand for Canterbury, England, and I took the liberty of telephoning. Your uncle told me about you and gave me your number in Porton. Dr Morgan, by the way, are you a doctor of medicine?
Dr Morgan I am a biochemist.
Dr Kirshner Ah! I see! Porton, of course, that is where the English work on chemical and bacteriological warfare, is it not?
Dr Morgan It is a research laboratory, that is all.
Dr Kirshner There is a possibility that I may be able to help your father if I knew a little more about him. You see he won't tell us anything.
Dr Morgan May I see him now?
Dr Kirshner You will be able to see him shortly, but I hope you won't mind telling me as much as you can about him first.
Dr Morgan Of course, but I've had no contact with him since I was a child. You know more about him than I do. You see I was away at a boarding school for girls when my mother... did you know about my mother?
Dr Kirshner Only that she was killed in an air-raid in Munich.
Dr Morgan A direct hit on our house in Veldtstrasse. My mother and my brother. It was just before the end of the war, in

nineteen forty-four. Father was working somewhere near Cracow at the time, in Poland. On munitions. I stayed on at school until nineteen forty-seven and then I went to live with my aunt.
Dr Kirshner In England?
Dr Morgan She had married an Englishman whom she met on holiday and gone to live with him in Canterbury. She died some years ago.
Dr Kirshner Didn't you write to your father?
Dr Morgan Every week. Then he stopped replying. Nineteen forty-nine it was. That was when I last heard from him. He seemed to have disappeared. My aunt went over to Germany to try and find him but she couldn't trace him. We presumed, eventually, that he had died.
Dr Kirshner And you?
Dr Morgan Me? I went to school in Canterbury, then to Cambridge, where I qualified. I was legally adopted by my aunt and uncle after father disappeared, and took their name.
Dr Kirshner And you never married?
Dr Morgan I am shortly to be married.
Dr Kirshner Strange, isn't it, that your father should break off contact with you? Did your aunt perhaps change her address?
Dr Morgan Oh no. Edward—that's my uncle—has a splendid old house in Canterbury, his family have lived there for over a hundred years.
Dr Kirshner Then severing connection with you was a deliberate act.
Dr Morgan It seems very much like it.
Dr Kirshner Can you think of any reason why he should do that?
Dr Morgan None whatever. I mean ... I'm astounded!

They contemplate each other in silence for a moment

This ... sanatorium ... it's a lunatic asylum, isn't it?
Dr Kirshner We don't use that terminology any longer. We call it an Institution of Mental Health.
Dr Morgan Is my father ... insane, Doctor?
Dr Kirshner (*slowly, after thought*) He seems to suffer from isolated and infrequent moments of insanity, during which he can become exceedingly violent.
Dr Morgan Violent?
Dr Kirshner I'm afraid so. It appears, as far as I can tell, to be a

schizophrenia, resulting in hallucinations or delusional ideas of some kind. Occasionally the delusions assume a reality for him and he becomes violent. Quite uncharacteristically, for he seems otherwise to be a gentle person.

Dr Morgan What form do these hallucinations take? And what causes them?

Dr Kirshner That is what I have been trying to discover. His pattern of behaviour is illogical. He gives us no trouble whatsoever, but there are strong reactions whenever one tries to probe into his background, which in his circumstances and with my responsibilities is of course inevitable.

Dr Morgan Is there anything I can do?

Dr Kirshner I feel that with a stable home background, if that were possible, I think I could recommend his release.

Dr Morgan I would be quite agreeable to take my father with me, of course, if that is what you are suggesting.

Dr Kirshner I am glad to hear you say that. The final decision regarding what happens to your father will not be made by me, he is still under the jurisdiction of the Court. My job is merely to report to them on his mental state.

Dr Morgan Oh!

Dr Kirshner You will understand that I have a responsibility to the public at large. As I explained briefly over the telephone, your father has been involved in sudden, vicious, unprovoked attacks on perfectly innocent people on several occasions.

Dr Morgan And you think it could occur again.

Dr Kirshner Think carefully, Dr Morgan, are you aware of anything that occurred whilst you were with your father which might explain these attacks?

Dr Morgan (*shaking her head slowly*) No ...

Dr Kirshner Anything, however apparently insignificant, which might have had some bearing on his inexplicable behaviour?

Dr Morgan No ... nothing ... not a thing.

Dr Kirshner Are you sure?

Dr Morgan I can think of nothing.

Dr Kirshner As a child—before the air-raid—try to remember.

Dr Morgan We were all very happy together.

Dr Kirshner What were your circumstances?

Dr Morgan (*not understanding*) Please?

Dr Kirshner Were you comfortably placed?

Dr Morgan Well, we lived on the Veldtstrasse, which as you probably know is a very good part of Munich. A large house it was, old, but very nice. At least that is how I remember it.
Dr Kirshner Did you have staff? Servants?
Dr Morgan We had a young girl. Later we had two, a woman also. Yes, we had two servants. Why?
Dr Kirshner So your father could afford the expense of a large house and two servants.
Dr Morgan I suppose he must have been able to. I've never thought about it. Why do you ask? My father is an honest man, Dr Kirshner, and he was well thought of as an engineer. Besides, the women didn't cost my mother anything, I seem to recall, just their food.
Dr Kirshner Were they two of the Russian women?
Dr Morgan I don't understand.
Dr Kirshner My family had one of the Russian women—they got no wages—I thought perhaps ...
Dr Morgan Perhaps they were. Yes, I remember now, neither of them spoke much German. They were also killed when the bomb fell.
Dr Kirshner And the house? Did your father buy it? Own it?
Dr Morgan As far as I remember it belonged to some people who had gone away. The authorities let us have it because my father was doing important work on armaments.
Dr Kirshner People who had gone away?
Dr Morgan The house had been left empty, but with all the furniture in it. There were quite a few in that neighbourhood.
Dr Kirshner Ah! Yes! I know what you mean.
Dr Morgan I remember mother saying there was no point in leaving them empty.
Dr Kirshner No, of course not. Tell me, Dr Morgan, did you at any time hear, from your aunt or anyone, whether there was any history of mental illness in the family?
Dr Morgan Good Lord no. I'm sure I would have heard if there had been. No, nothing whatever.
Dr Kirshner Then I think I need no longer keep you from meeting your father again.
Dr Morgan Does he ... know that I'm here?
Dr Kirshner Not yet. I'll have him brought here. (*She presses the button on her desk*)

Asylum

Dr Morgan May I not see him privately?

Dr Kirshner Later. But if you don't mind, I would like to be present when you meet.

Dr Morgan (*doubtfully*) If you think it will help you.

The Secretary enters

Dr Kirshner Would you tell Metz to bring Herr Bauermann to my room please?

The Secretary exits

How old were you when you last saw him, Dr Morgan?

Dr Morgan I was eleven. I went to England when I was eleven.

Dr Kirshner And that was two years after ...

Dr Morgan After my mother died? Yes. I was nine when that happened.

Dr Kirshner In those two years, between nine and eleven, how did you get on with your father? Well?

Dr Morgan I noticed nothing unusual. I was away at school of course and father worked in Poland at first. Then they moved him nearer home, because of me.

Dr Kirshner What about the holidays? Did you come home?

Dr Morgan My father got special permission for me to stay on at school during the holidays. You see we had no home at that time. He came to see me weekends, when he could. We were promised a flat in Munich as soon as possible, but there were many worse cases than ours. That's mainly why I was sent to live with my aunt—you see I had to leave boarding school when I was eleven.

There is a knock at the door

Dr Kirshner Come in.

Metz ushers in Bauermann. He glances at his daughter but does not recognize her and stands, looking down

Dr Morgan rises

Thank you, Metz. Would you wait in the outer office.

Metz leaves

Herr Bauermann ...

No response

   Herr Bauermann, this lady is your daughter.

Bauermann looks up at her slowly, then over to his daughter

Dr Morgan Hello, Father ...

Bauermann stands looking at her with a hardening expression, almost reaching one of hate

   Father—I'm Lisa.
Bauermann Lisa?

He stares at his daughter, then looks at Dr Kirshner with abhorrence, then back to his daughter

Bauermann What are ... ? Who ... ?
Dr Morgan Why didn't you answer my letters?
Bauermann How did you ... ?
Dr Kirshner *I* traced your daughter, Herr Bauermann. Never mind how. Aren't you glad to see her?
Bauermann You ... traced ... her ... !? You. ... ?

Suddenly he springs upon Dr Kirshner, his hands round her neck

Dr Kirshner (*choking*) Metz! Metz!
Dr Morgan Father! What are you doing? Father!

Bauermann brings the doctor to the floor. His daughter tries to drag him off

   Metz and the Secretary, hearing Dr Kirshner's screams, rush in, and the three of them struggle with Bauermann, but not very successfully

As they struggle the Lights fade and the music starts

Scene 3

The same. Night

The room is lit by two lamps, one on the desk and one by the centre chair, leaving the rest of the room in darkness. Dr Kirshner is

Asylum

working at her desk. Around her neck, which has bruise marks, is a silk handkerchief

Metz enters, carrying a tray with a hypodermic syringe, etc. The music fades

Dr Kirshner Pentathyamol?
Metz Five hundred milligrams, like you said.
Dr Kirshner Good. How is he?
Metz Calm.
Dr Kirshner Still crying?
Metz Ever since. Hasn't stopped. Day and night.
Dr Kirshner Has he had his injection?
Metz No, you said not ...
Dr Kirshner Good. Any tablets?
Metz No.
Dr Kirshner All right. You can bring him in now. Then leave.
Metz Leave?
Dr Kirshner Yes, leave.
Metz Are you sure?
Dr Kirshner (*sternly*) Do as I say, Metz!
Metz Yes, Frau Doctor.

Metz exits

Dr Kirshner goes over to the tray, examines the small bottle, inserts the hypodermic needle and draws up the liquid carefully testing for air bubbles

Metz enters with a docile but tear-stained, red-eyed Bauermann and sits him in a chair, centre, facing forward

Dr Kirshner Roll up his sleeve.

Metz does so. There is no resistance from Bauermann

This is just a sedative, Herr Bauermann. Make you feel better. (*To Metz*) Hold his arm.

She injects Bauermann's arm, slowly while he continues to look straight ahead

Thank you, Metz.
Metz Don't you think I should stay?

She looks at him sharply

Reluctantly Metz leaves

Dr Kirshner Now. How are we today?

There is a long pause during which she observes him, occasionally looking at her watch

Bauermann (*quietly*) I ... I am sorry for what I did ... to you ... Doctor. I don't know what came over me.
Dr Kirshner And I didn't know you were so strong, Herr Bauermann. That's quite a grip for a man of your age.
Bauermann Where is ... my daughter? I thought she would ...
Dr Kirshner She went back to England.
Bauermann Ah. I'm glad.
Dr Kirshner Weren't you pleased to see her?
Bauermann She looks ... a fine young woman.
Dr Kirshner She's a research chemist. A doctor.
Bauermann (*impressed*) So!

Bauermann rubs himself where he received the injection

Dr Kirshner Is it painful?
Bauermann It feels a little ... it will be all right.
Dr Kirshner Herr Bauermann ... why did you attack me?

Bauermann's face very slowly hardens

Weren't you happy that I was able to trace your daughter for you?
Bauermann I ... I don't like people who ... interfere with other people. I don't like it when one person ... interferes in another person's life. A man's life is his own. Nobody else's. People have no right ... do this, do that ... work! Run! March! Lie in the mud! ... live! ... die! ...

He pauses with his eyes closed for a moment

Trace her? What do you mean trace her? She wasn't lost. I knew her address. I knew where she was. All the time I kept her ... I could have ... at any time I could have ... if I'd wanted to. You had no right! What business of yours ... ? Who gave you the right ... ?
Dr Kirshner I was trying to help you.

Bauermann Who wants you to help me? Have I asked you ... ? What's it got to do with you if ... ? She's *my* daughter, not yours! *My* daughter!

Dr Kirshner I thought ...

Bauermann (*raising his voice*) She was in England! She got away from this place! I got her away! Why can't you ... ?

Dr Kirshner I'm sorry, Herr Bauermann. Perhaps it was wrong of me.

Bauermann How old are you, Doctor?

Dr Kirshner (*surprised*) Why?

Bauermann Always why! No whys! How old are you?

Dr Kirshner That doesn't concern you!

Bauermann But you saw.

Dr Kirshner I don't understand.

Bauermann You *saw*. You were old enough to see. To understand.

Dr Kirshner Saw what? What are you talking about?

Bauermann My god! What am I talking about! How quickly you can forget!

Dr Kirshner I don't understand ... what are you referring to?

Bauermann Never mind. Never mind.

Dr Kirshner Was it the air-raid?

There is a pause. Bauermann rubs his arm

Bauermann Do you remember ... the lines of people, being pushed along the street ... led away ... women and children ... old men ... babies even ... led away by men in uniform ... with guns? Germans ... ordinary Germans ... like you and me ... not even at night, in the daytime, for all to see. Going ... god knows where ... to slave labour ... to gas chambers ... to be murdered ... thousands and thousands and thousands! And we saw this. We saw this! You and me, we *saw* this. And we turned our backs ... and we walked on ... as if it wasn't happening.

He pauses, in thought

And we took their things, their possessions, their houses, their homes ... from our neighbours we took their things ... and from other countries, our neighbouring countries, we took their food ... their men ... their women even. And nobody said a word. Not a word. (*He smiles*) We *cheered*. And we waved. And we felt good, and proud. (*The smile dies*) And we watched the lines of people being led away with their pitiful little bundles ... prodded and cursed and driven on by the men with guns ... men like me ... and we said nothing ...

Dr Kirshner (*a sudden revelation*) Is that why you ... ? The schoolmaster?

Bauermann (*his mouth curls into a sneer*) He was herding them along, herding the children along, shouting at them, goading them ...

Dr Kirshner My god.

Bauermann I couldn't bear it ...

Dr Kirshner (*after a pause*) But the foreman you attacked ... you were his superior, he wasn't a foreman over you?

Bauermann A little rat! Some kind of god he thought he was! Do you know where I was working in nineteen forty-two and nineteen forty-three and nineteen forty-four? I was working in a factory near Cracow. I was in charge of my part of the factory. There were French workers, and Dutch, and Russians, and Jews, and Poles ... all sorts ... slaves. All slaves. Without pay. Fourteen hours a day they worked! Sometimes even sixteen! We could beat them, kick them, if they weren't working fast enough, take them outside and kill them, if we wanted to. We Germans felt so ... powerful! Important! Big! Superior! And there were brothels for us. Yes, for the overseers and the bosses—but not for Poles, only for Germans. With the girls! We could do whatever we wanted with them ... for free ... and we went there ... and we laughed ... not thinking ... not caring ...

There is a pause

And down the road from the factory ... a few kilometres ... was Birkenau. Birkenau! And we saw the cattle trucks arriving every day. So packed with people we wouldn't treat animals even, like that. Day after day. I saw. Everybody saw. And we saw the smoke from the chimneys ... and when we went for a walk on the Sundays we could smell the burning flesh ... and we all knew ... I knew, you knew ... and we said nothing ... not a word!

Dr Kirshner Herr Bauermann ... you cannot take it upon yourself to be the conscience of Germany ...

Bauermann (*not hearing her*) When the bombs fell I wasn't surprised. I began to realize ... we deserved it. We earned it. (*He* *pauses*) The pity was our children ... our own children ... Eckhart! Little Eckhart! (*He cries*) But the other children! We did it to the other children, didn't we? Even the most bestial barbarians in history spared the little children. But we ... we watched, and saw ... the little children ... we earned everything.

Dr Kirshner You must try and forget, Herr Bauermann. We must all try to forget. You cannot live with it forever.

Bauermann I try. I try to forget ... like everyone ... to behave as though we didn't ... then suddenly ... something takes me back ... somebody behaves like ... (*His face hardens*) and I can't stand it! I can't stand it!

He cries. She puts an arm around his shoulder

Dr Kirshner Try to be calm. Don't distress yourself ...

Bauermann And then ... when we were beaten ... (*a note of wonder comes into his voice*) everyone shrugged it off! All of a sudden nobody knew! Nobody had seen! Everybody was innocent! Even today, the head of the slave factory where I was working in Cracow ... he's wealthy. Respected. In the Government. As if he wasn't ... it was happening all around us, but nobody had seen ... speak to anybody, everything was done by somebody else, somebody *else*. Always somebody else.

Dr Kirshner All that is in the past, Herr Bauermann. We must forget ...

Bauermann The young people say to us ... how could you have done it? And we reply, "but *we* didn't do it". I say whoever did it, we did it because we tolerated it. *Enjoyed* it even!

Dr Kirshner It was a bad chapter in our history, but we must forget about the Nazis.

Bauermann (*angrily*) To hell with the Nazis! It is *myself* I cannot forget! It is *myself* I cannot forgive! I am just as guilty as ... as you are ... everybody ...

Dr Kirshner (*after a pause*) Why did you not let your daughter know where you were?

Bauermann Lisa. She was an only child. I didn't want her to be ... better she should be somewhere else. I didn't want her to be ... like us! Like me ... and like you and everybody that thinks like you. (*Cynically*) It is all in the past, forget, forget!

Dr Kirshner (*slowly and quietly*) But we *must* forget ... to remain sane.

Bauermann Sane? Sane? Don't you understand, *outside* is the asylum. A great asylum full of lunatics. They haven't the sense to learn. Wherever you look they are busy killing each other. Do sane people behave like that? Wherever you look, ordering each other about ... kidnapping ... torturing ... planting bombs ... making big bombs, hydrogen bombs, god knows what new horrors they are thinking up ... for other people ... but in the end for themselves. The governments, the people, the scientists ... all together. They're mad! Insane! And you say forget! *I say remember! Remember!* I don't want to forget. To forget is insane. I want to stay sane ... and remember ...

There is a long pause. Dr Kirshner presses the button

Dr Kirshner Sometimes, Herr Bauermann, it is necessary to be mad with the rest of the world rather than be wise alone.

Metz enters

Metz (*aside to Dr Kirshner*) Did the Pentathyamol work, Frau Doctor?

Dr Kirshner (*immersed in her own thoughts*) Eh?

Metz Did he ... open up?

She nods

Well?

Dr Kirshner (*pulling herself together; aside to Metz*) Pronounced obsessional paranoia I'm afraid, Metz.

Metz Thought so.

Dr Kirshner He is not only clearly insane within the legal definition of insanity, but worse than that—he's dangerous, I regret to say. He could do a great deal of harm to a great many people. I'll admit him as a permanent resident. It is quite unsafe to return him to society.

She goes over to Bauermann and places a hand on his shoulder

Metz will take you back to your room now, Herr Bauermann. Have a good night's rest. You'll feel better in the morning.

As Metz takes Bauermann out the music starts quietly

Dr Kirshner goes to her desk and closes the file with Bauermann's case history. She puts it in a drawer and shakes her head

The Lights fade as the music swells

CURTAIN

FURNITURE AND PROPERTY LIST

On stage: Desk. *On it:* telephone, bell button, lamp, ruler, case history
Chairs
Lamp

Off stage: Files **(Secretary)**
Notes **(Probation Officer)**
Tray *On it:* hypodermic syringe, bottle etc. (Metz)

Personal: **Bauermann:** wallet containing photograph
Dr Kirshner: watch

EFFECTS PLOT

Cue 1	**Dr Kirshner** "Take him away!" *Music, quietly*	(Page 9)
Cue 2	**Dr Kirshner** makes a gesture of extreme frustration *Music swells*	(Page 9)
Cue 3	To open Scene 2 *Music fades*	(Page 10)
Cue 4	They struggle with **Bauermann**. As they struggle *Music*	(Page 16)
Cue 5	To open Scene 3 *Music fades*	(Page 16)
Cue 6	**Metz** takes **Bauermann** out *Music, quietly*	(Page 22)
Cue 7	**Dr Kirshner** shakes her head *Music swells*	(Page 22)

LIGHTING PLOT

To open: General interior lighting

Cue 1   **Dr Kirshner** makes a gesture of extreme frustration   (Page 9)
Fade to black-out

Scene 2
Cue 2   As music fades   (Page 10)
Bring up Lights for scene 2

Cue 3   They struggle with **Bauermann**. As they struggle   (Page 16)
Fade to black-out

Scene 3
Cue 4   As music fades   (Page 16)
Bring up lamps and covering spots for scene 3

Cue 5   **Dr Kirshner** shakes her head   (Page 22)
Fade to black-out

www.ingramcontent.com/pod-product-compliance
Lightning Source LLC
Chambersburg PA
CBHW070455050426
42450CB00012B/3286